TEMPLES IN TIME

Written by Vaishali Batra
Illustrated by Naomi Skinner

OXFORD
UNIVERSITY PRESS

Words to look out for ...

accuse (*verb*)
accuses, accusing, accused
To accuse someone is to say that they did something wrong.

celebrate (*verb*)
celebrates, celebrating, celebrated
If you celebrate, you do something special to show that something is important.

compassion (*noun*)
Compassion is care or pity that you show to people or animals that are suffering.

contrast (*noun*)
a clear difference

deny (*verb*)
deny, denying, denied
to not allow someone to have something

enable (*verb*)
enables, enabling, enabled
to make it possible for someone or something to do something

instinct (*noun*)
If your instinct is to do something, you can do it without thinking about it and without being told what to do.

persist (*verb*)
persists, persisting, persisted
to last for a long time

reasonable (*adjective*)
sensible or logical

thorough (*adjective*)
done properly and carefully

Contents

Your trip starts here ...

Imagine you could fly a drone high above your home. What would it show you?

You would probably see many kinds of new and old buildings. They might be houses, shops, schools, restaurants, offices and places of **worship**.

Some buildings may look similar. Others may have impressive features that make them stand out.

Many old buildings are still standing even today. Their walls may be worn or have fallen down, but they can hold fascinating stories from the past.

Throughout history, humans have shown an instinct to build. At first, they made simple buildings using what was around them, like rocks, stones and wood. Over time, they began making more complicated buildings using clever designs. Some of the most amazing buildings from the past are temples.

A temple is a building made for people who follow a particular **religion**. Those people gather there to show respect and worship together. Different religions have different kinds of temples.

Imagine that your drone could fly anywhere in the world – or even back in time! Let's send it to go and see some of the most amazing ancient temples.

If your instinct is to do something, you can do it without thinking about it and without being told what to do.

Ancient Egyptian temples

First, imagine that your drone is flying over northern Africa. You see large stone structures that were built by ancient Egyptian people. These structures are what is left of ancient temples.

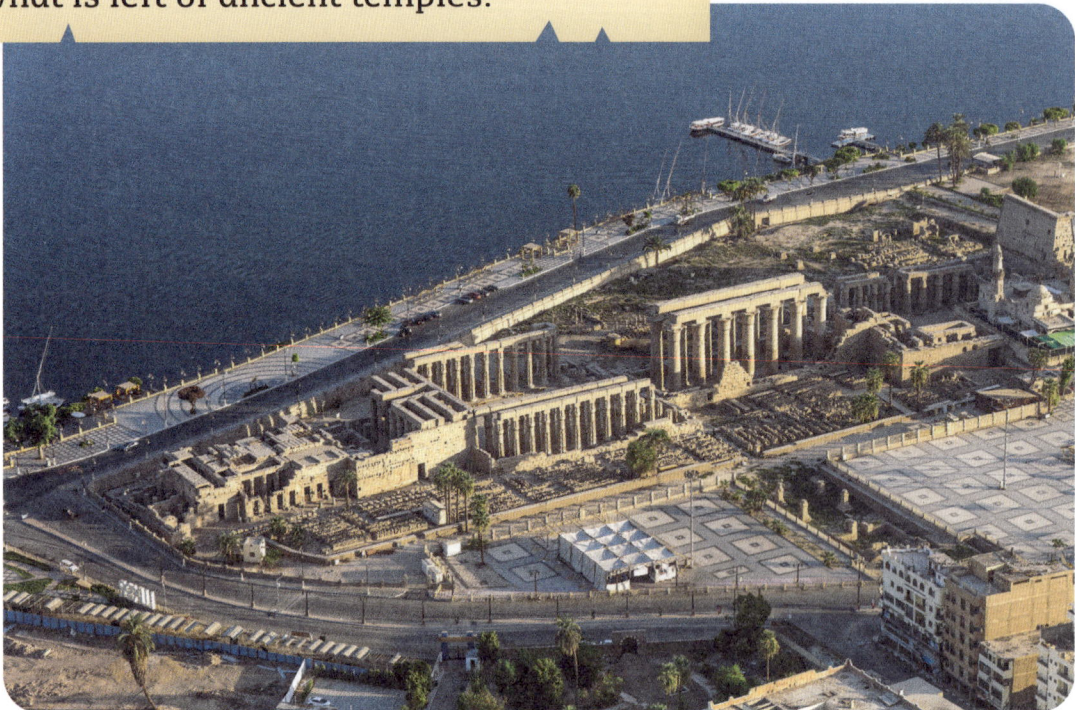

The temples were built thousands of years ago. Each temple was built to praise a god or **pharaoh** (say: *fair-roh*).

The temples were looked after by priests. Being an ancient Egyptian priest meant you were very powerful and respected. The main duty of a temple priest was to serve the god.

Experts think that ordinary ancient Egyptian people may have been denied entry to some temples.

If you are denied something, you are not allowed to have it.

Ancient Egyptian temples were large, complicated structures that were built over many years.

Stone walls were built around the temple area.

There were rows of columns that were often carved with pictures.

Large gateways formed the entrances.

courtyard

The temples had statues inside.

Temples had different zones such as courtyards and halls. Many temples also had lakes and gardens. Some temples even had libraries and kitchens!

The most important area of the temple was the inner **sanctuary**. This was where the statue of the temple's main god was placed.

Some pharaohs made thorough plans for temples to be built for them after they had died.

If something is thorough, it is done properly and carefully.

Karnak temple

The largest ancient temple group in Egypt is at Karnak. It is believed that about 30 different pharaohs built it, over many hundreds of years.

The three temple areas that you can still see today were for three ancient Egyptian gods.

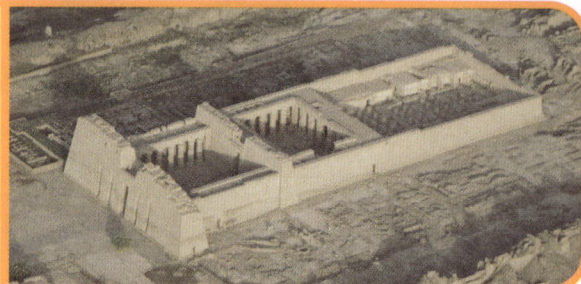

The main area of the temple group lies in the centre. It features the Great Temple of Amun.

The building's design works with the direction of the sun in the sky. On 21st December every year, sunlight shines through a gate and enters Amun's **shrine**.

Great Temple of Amun

The Great Temple of Amun was built to be the god Amun's home on earth.

The walls inside the temple are covered with carvings. They show special events taking place, such as religious **ceremonies**.

The temple has rows of large statues leading to its entrance. Each statue has the head of a ram and the body of a lion.

The hall in the centre of the temple contains 134 massive columns. The largest 12 columns are a dizzying 24 metres high!

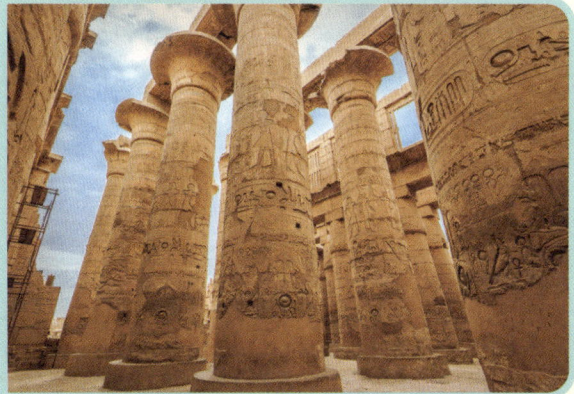

The Temples of Abu Simbel

Thousands of years ago, two ancient Egyptian temples were built near the River Nile in southern Egypt. However, over time, one was almost entirely hidden by sand. It was dug up in 1813, after an explorer stumbled across the tops of its statues!

Both temples are decorated with carvings and statues of a pharaoh and his family.

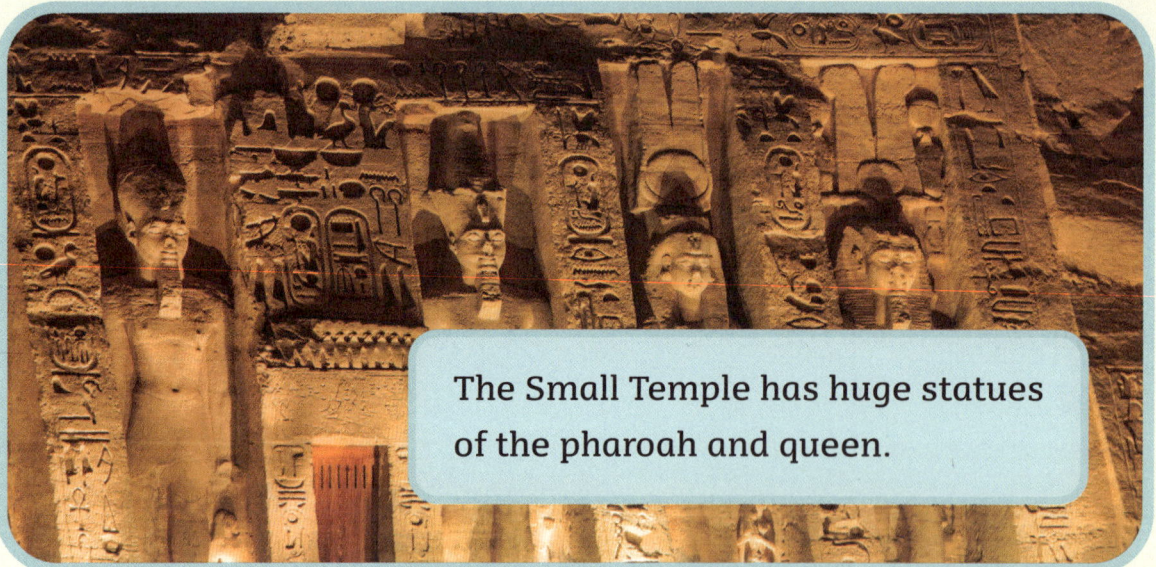

The Small Temple has huge statues of the pharoah and queen.

The Great Temple was built in line with the direction of the sun. On 22nd February and 22nd October, sunlight enters the inner sanctuary to light up the statues.

In the 1960s, there was a risk that the River Nile would flood the two temples.

A team of engineers and scientists made a plan. They saw that there was only one reasonable way to save them.

They had to move the temples to higher ground.

Both temples were carefully taken apart. The rocks were sliced into hundreds of blocks. Each block weighed a huge 20–30 tonnes.

The blocks were transported to the new place and joined back together! The engineers made sure to copy the original temples exactly.

If something is reasonable, it is sensible or logical.

Ancient Greek temples

Next, your drone flies north, towards Europe. It reaches Greece and the city of Athens. On top of a hill above the city, you see the remains of ancient temples. This collection of temples is the 'Acropolis' (say: *uh-crop-uh-liss*).

The temples that still stand on the Acropolis today were built on top of older temples that had been destroyed. Some stories accuse fighting armies of destroying the older temples. Others blame earthquakes.

On the Acropolis there is a temple for Athena, the Greek goddess of **wisdom**. She was often shown with an owl. Owls might have become linked to wisdom because they were her symbol. They aren't really that clever!

To accuse someone is to say that they did something wrong.

Almost all ancient Greek temples were rectangular in shape. Many had similar designs.

Today, we see only the bare stone of ruined temples. However, they were originally painted in bright colours.

Their roofs were made of tiles.

At each end, sculptures decorated a triangular area called a 'pediment'.

A decorative strip called a 'frieze' extended around the building.

Rows of columns lined the sides.

Steps led up to the temple's floor level.

The statue of the temple's god or goddess was in a room inside the temple.

Friezes often showed scenes from Greek **myths**.

The Parthenon

The Parthenon (say: *par-the-non*) is the largest temple in the Acropolis. Over time, it has been damaged by wars, fire and theft. Some parts of it were taken to different museums. However, the main structure has persisted.

Its most amazing feature was its frieze, which shows scenes of ceremonies held for the ancient Greek goddess Athena.

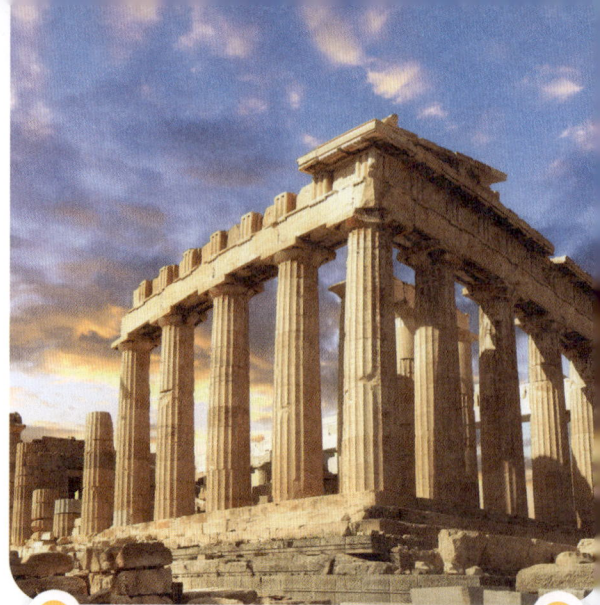

The Parthenon is about 30 metres wide and 70 metres long.

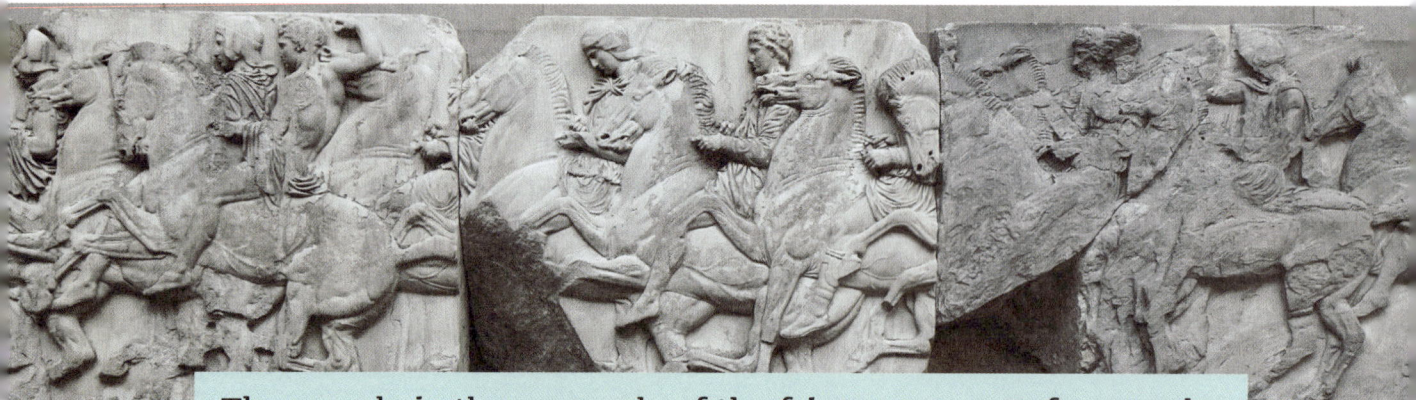

The people in these panels of the frieze are part of a parade.

Inside the temple, there was once a large statue of Athena made of **ivory** and gold. Records suggest it was about twelve metres tall. That's around the height of three buses stacked on top of each other!

To persist is to last for a long time.

The Erechtheion

The Erechtheion (say: *ih-rek-thee-on*) was a temple built to show the power of Athens. It was built for Poseidon, the ancient Greek god of the sea, as well as for Athena.

A myth explains why the temple was built in this place.

Poseidon and Athena both wanted loyalty from the people of Athens. They decided to compete for it by each offering a gift.

Poseidon smashed his spear into the land and sea water flowed from the ground. Athena planted a branch, and it quickly grew into an olive tree.

In contrast to salty water, the tree's olives would be useful. The people of Athens chose Athena's gift. They built the Erechtheion beside it.

A tree still stands there today!

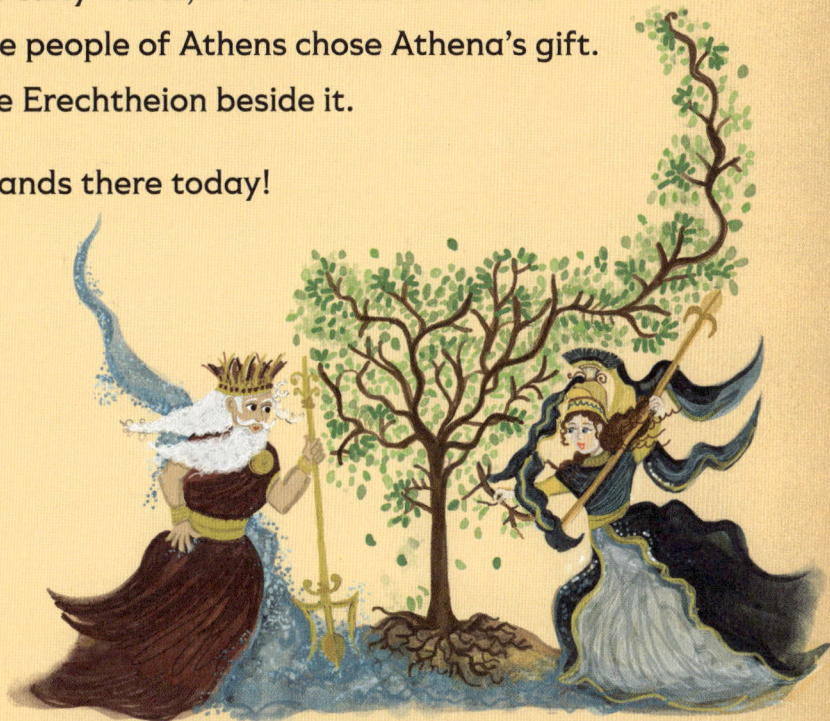

Contrast is a clear difference. The phrase 'in contrast to' is used when saying that someone or something is very different from another person or thing.

The main part of the Erechtheion is divided into two rooms. One room used to contain a statue of Athena holding a shield.

Two of the temple's three porches are supported by columns.

A **sacred** olive tree grows outside.

The third porch has six statues of women. They look like they are supporting the roof on their heads. That's some heavy lifting!

The temple was built on bumpy ground, so one side is three metres lower than the other.

Mesoamerican temples

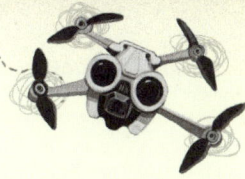

Send your drone across the Atlantic ocean, towards Central America. You can see many impressive temples from ancient Mesoamerica.

Mesoamerica is an area of central America. For thousands of years, groups of people called the Olmec, Zapotec, Maya, Toltec and Aztec lived there.

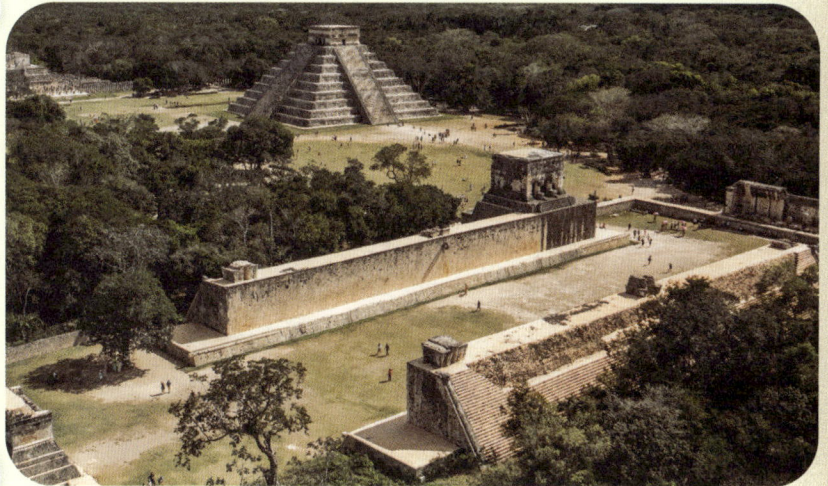

Many Mesoamerican temples were built in the shape of a pyramid, but with multiple steps. They were decorated with carvings of detailed shapes and patterns. Some temples were built keeping in mind the position of the sun, moon and stars in the sky.

This carving shows an Aztec god shaped like a snake with feathers.

Temple of Kukulkan

Zoom in on the ruins of an ancient city in Mexico. This large step pyramid is called the Temple of Kukulkan.

The temple was for Kukulkan, a Mayan snake god.

The structure was built in stages, over centuries.

The temple's extraordinary design displays the Mayan calendar. Each side has 91 steps, making 365 steps altogether – one for each day of the year.

Twice a year, a shadow falls on the pyramid in the shape of a snake.

The Temple of Kukulkan is also called 'El Castillo', which means 'The Castle'.

The Pyramid of the Sun

Let's fly your drone to another ancient city in Mexico. The Aztec people called this 'the place where gods were created'. It is the home of the Pyramid of the Sun, made of rocks from volcanoes.

At the top of the pyramid is a flat platform. This may have been used to celebrate religious occasions.

The pyramid has several levels that rise to the top.

The Pyramid of the Sun is more than 60 metres tall. It covers an area of 50 600 square metres. That's about the height of a 20-storey building and the area of 10 football fields!

There are mysterious tunnels under the pyramid. Remains of clay pots, glass, animal bones and carved models have been found there.

If you celebrate, you do something special to show that something is important.

Mesopotamian temples

Change your drone's direction towards Asia. As it comes down in west Asia, you can see remains of Mesopotamian temples.

Mesopotamia was a large area of land in the Middle East. In the past, many different groups of people lived there.

These temples are called 'ziggurats' (say: *zig-uh-rats*). Ziggurats look like massive stepped pyramids with flat tops. They were made of mud bricks. At the top of a ziggurat, there was a temple for a god or goddess.

Most people could only access the lower levels of the ziggurat. It is believed that priests would <u>deny</u> people access to the top.

Many ziggurats have been destroyed or damaged over time, but some still remain.

If you are <u>denied</u> something, you are not allowed to have it.

Great Ziggurat of Ur

The remains of the largest ziggurat are in what is now Iraq. It is called the Great Ziggurat of Ur. Experts believe it was built around 4000 years ago.

At the top was a temple for the moon god Nanna.

A series of levels were built with mud bricks.

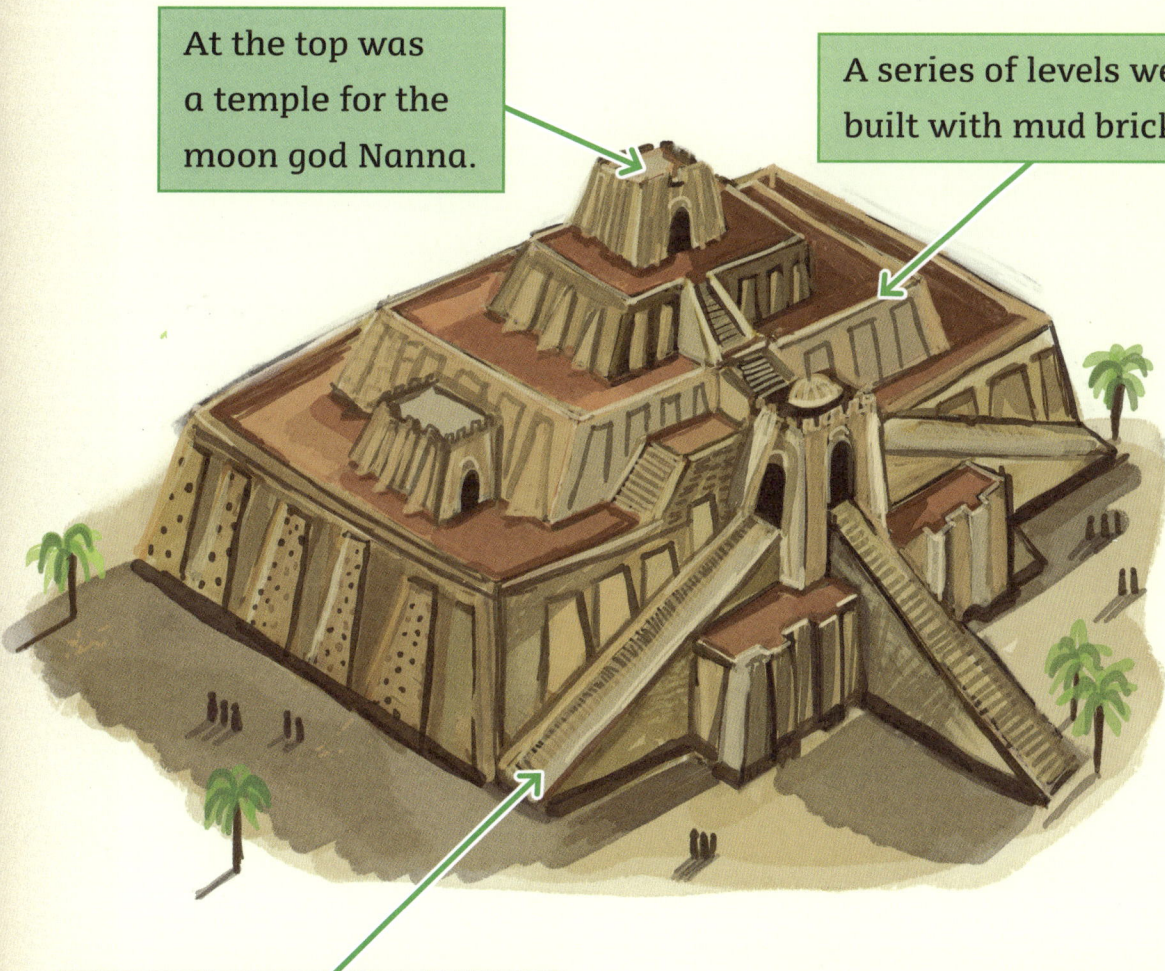

A staircase enabled people to climb up the ziggurat.

The Great Ziggurat of Ur was part of a temple group.

Experts think the Great Ziggurat of Ur used to be over 30 metres tall. It might have been a symbol of the ruler's power and wealth.

To enable someone or something to do something is to make it possible for them to do it.

Ancient Temples in India

Steer your drone further east, towards India. You will be able to fly down to see some of the most extraordinary temples ever built.

This temple is an ancient Hindu temple. Hinduism is one of the world's oldest religions. It is the religion of many people around the world today.

Many ancient Hindu temples had similar designs. These would include features like a shrine, a sanctum (inner hall), one or more towers (tall structures) and a porch (an open hall where people **pray**). They were often built to face the rising sun.

The Sun Temple in Konark

The Sun Temple in Konark was built for the Hindu sun god Surya. It is decorated with carvings of musicians, dancers and animals.

The entrance of the temple gets the first rays of the sun at dawn.

The Sun Temple in Konark was designed to represent the sun god's **chariot**.

There are 24 carved wheels like this one, to represent the 24 hours of the day.

Seven carved horses seem to pull the temple along. They represent the seven days of the week.

Vittala temple

Turning south, zoom in to see the Vittala temple group in Hampi. This is another ancient Hindu temple.

The most impressive feature of the temple is the Stone Chariot. It looks like it's carved out of a single block of stone!

The temple group is surrounded by a high wall.

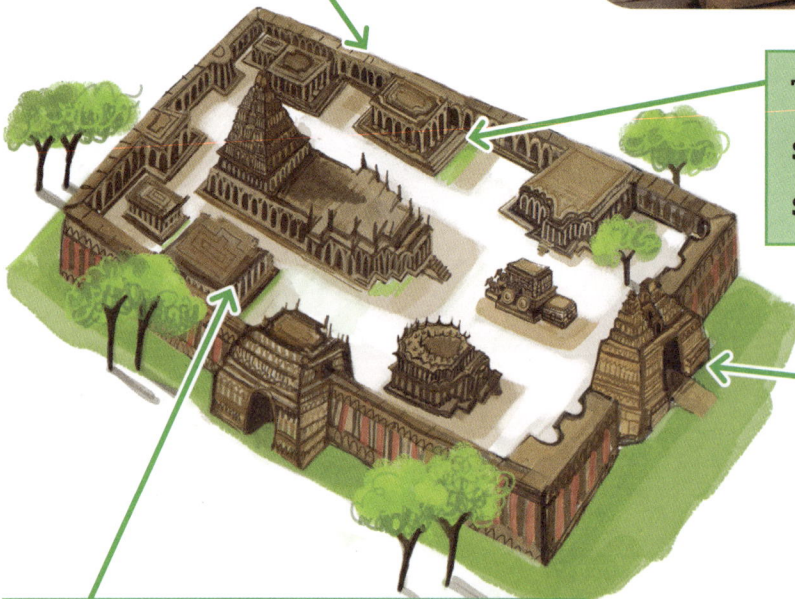

The main temple is surrounded by smaller shrines and courtyards.

Its large gateway is decorated with carvings and sculptures.

The temple group has halls with pillars decorated with carvings of gods and goddesses.

One particular hall has 56 carved pillars. They produce different musical notes when they are hit!

Cave temples

In many parts of the world, temples were carved out of solid natural rock. Builders often carved out from caves that already existed. They didn't have to build up walls, or carry heavy blocks of stone to the site!

The designs of cave temples often work alongside the natural features of the caves. They sometimes have detailed carvings around their entrances. These might include statues of gods, goddesses and other mythical figures.

Some of the oldest rock-cut buildings are the Barabar caves in India. Some surfaces in these caves have been polished so smoothly that they look almost like glass.

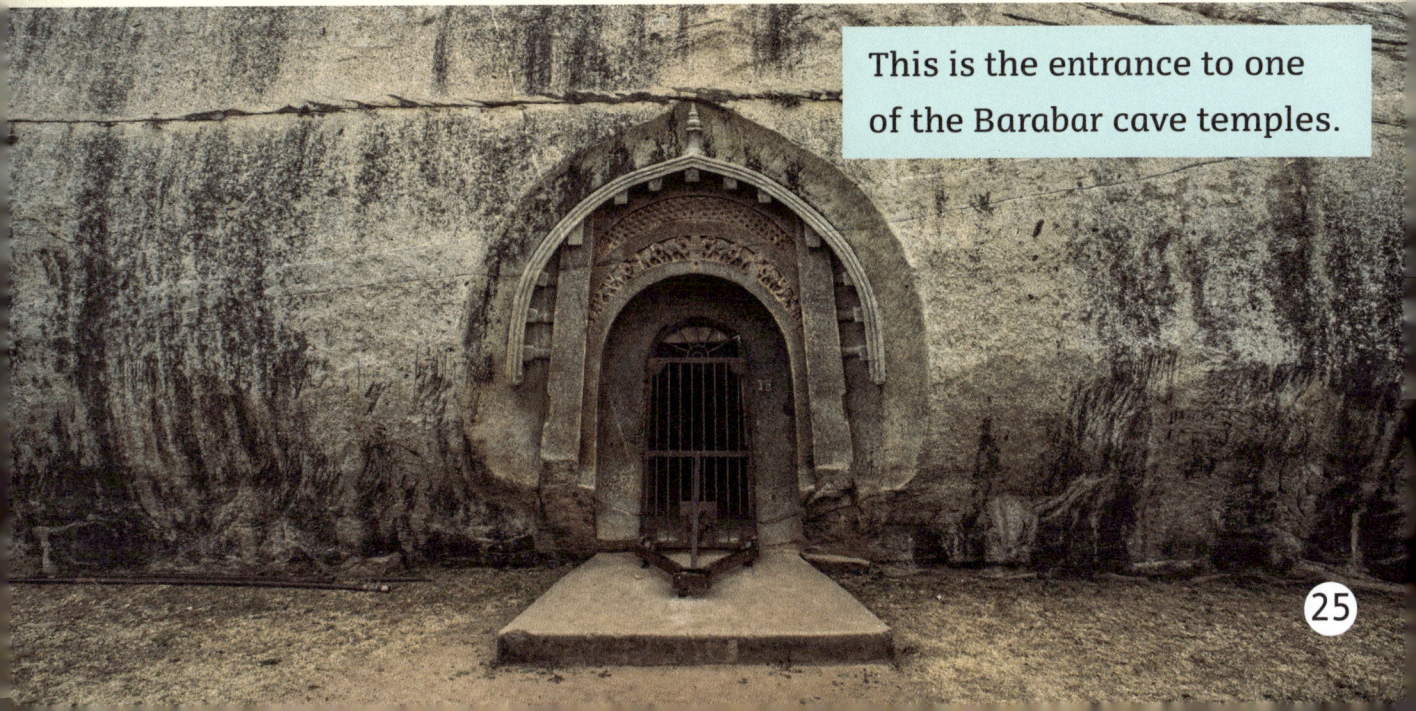

This is the entrance to one of the Barabar cave temples.

Kailasa temple

The Ellora Caves in India are a group of 34 rock-cut temples. They were carved over a period of more than 600 years.

They include temples for different religious beliefs, including Hinduism and Buddhism.

Buddhism is a religion followed by many people around the world today. It began in India over 2500 years ago.

The caves include the Kailasa temple, which was built over a period of more than 100 years. It is the world's largest structure cut out of solid rock.

a three-storey-high tower with a dome

It is covered in beautiful carvings and sculptures.

An ancient temple in Sri Lanka

The Royal Rock temple group

Let's fly our drone south and swoop down to see the Royal Rock temple group of Dambulla, in Sri Lanka. It includes five rock-cut temples.

The cave temples' ceilings are painted with detailed patterns along the rock surface. Their walls feature more than 150 statues and paintings of Buddha, who is the most important person in the Buddhist religion. It is believed that the Buddha images were first carved there over 2000 years ago.

The temples are at the base of a 150-metre-high rock. The largest cave entrance measures about 52 metres across.

The world's biggest temple!

Fly your drone further east, to Cambodia. Coming into view is Angkor Wat (say: *an-kor wah-t*), the world's largest religious temple group.

'Angkor Wat' means 'City of Temples'. It was built for a Hindu god called Vishnu. Later, it became a Buddhist temple. It is believed that about 300 000 people helped to build it – and 6000 elephants!

Angkor Wat has temples and galleries.

The main temple has five towers. These represent the five peaks of an important mountain.

It was protected by a **moat** and wall.

This bridge is 188 metres long!

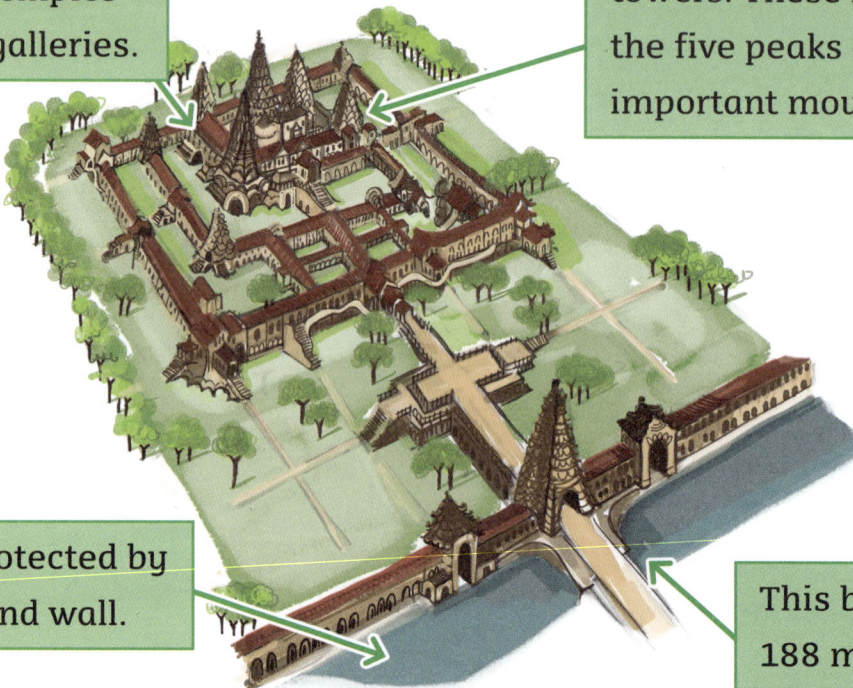

Modern temples

Many places of worship around the world have been built in more recent times. Some were inspired by ancient temples. Others have modern styles.

As it travels, your drone might fly over some amazing modern temples, too.

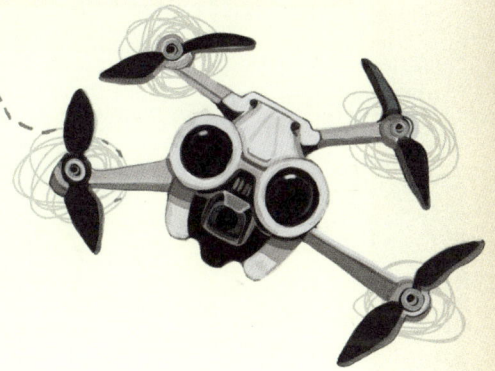

The Lotus Temple

The Bahá'í (say: *bar-hai*) House of Worship in India is known as the Lotus Temple. It is shaped like a lotus flower.

This Bahá'í temple offers a place for everyone to worship, as well as space to be calm and thoughtful. It encourages visitors to show respect for all faiths and compassion for all people.

Compassion is care or pity that you show to people or animals that are suffering.

Hechal Yehuda Synagogue

Hechal Yehuda **Synagogue** is a temple in Israel. It is designed to look like a seashell. The shape enables everyone inside to see and hear speakers from wherever they are seated.

The Golden Dome Mosque

The Golden Dome **Mosque** is in Indonesia. It has five domes coated with gleaming gold. The mosque can fit 20000 people in it.

Your drone has now flown all over the world. It's shown you temples in places as far apart as Mexico and Cambodia. It's zoomed through more than 4000 years of history!

Every temple has a story to tell. What do you think modern temples might tell people of the future about us?

To enable someone or something to do something is to make it possible for them to do it.

Glossary

ceremonies: sets of particular actions to celebrate or respect a special occasion

chariot: a vehicle with wheels, pulled by horses

courtyard: an open space that is surrounded by walls but has no roof

ivory: a hard, creamy-white substance made from the tusks or teeth of an animal, often an elephant

moat: a band of water around a building or town, designed to protect it

mosque: a building where Muslim people pray and worship

myths: traditional stories that may or may not be true

pharaoh: a ruler in ancient Egypt

pray: send thoughts and ideas towards, or to respect, a god

religion: a set of ideas and beliefs that people have about a god or gods

sacred: regarded with respect by a particular religion or group of people

sanctuary: a sacred place, often a particularly safe one

shrine: a sacred display or space closely connected to a god, where people can worship them and give offerings

synagogue: a building where Jewish people pray and worship

wisdom: the ability to act in a good and right way, and give good advice, because of experience and knowledge

worship: a way of respecting a god or a sacred ruler, often by praying

Index